THE LITTLE BOOK OF
BIG LAUGHS

DONNA CLARK GOODRICH

HARVEST HOUSE PUBLISHERS
EUGENE, OREGON

Cover by Dugan Design Group, Bloomington, Minnesota

Cover illustration © Dugan Design Group

THE LITTLE BOOK OF BIG LAUGHS

Copyright © 2014 by Donna Goodrich
Published by Harvest House Publishers
Eugene, Oregon 97402
www.harvesthousepublishers.com

ISBN 978-0-7369-5902-5 (pbk.)
ISBN 978-0-7369-5903-2 (eBook)

Printed in the United States of America

14 15 16 17 18 19 20 21 22 / BP-JH / 10 9 8 7 6 5 4 3 2 1

Ancestry

"My family can trace its ancestry back to William the Conqueror," said the boastful young man.

"I suppose," said his friend, "next you'll be telling us your ancestors were in the Ark with Noah."

"Of course not," said the first man. "My people had a boat of their own."

An illustrious New England family hired their lawyer to trace their ancestry. After months of research, he found that one member of the family had been convicted of a crime and hung. Not wanting to embarrass the family, he wrote this as the cause of death: "John was standing on a platform when it suddenly gave way."

Mrs. Cabot hired a genealogist to work up an impressive family tree for her. His research revealed that one ancestor had been electrocuted for murder, so he wrote of that person, "Occupied the chair of applied electricity at one of our better-known public institutions."

A hostess was trying to impress her party guests. "My family's ancestry is very old," she bragged. "It dates back to the days of King John of England." Then, turning to a lady sitting quietly in a corner, she asked condescendingly, "And how old is your family, my dear?"

"Well," said the woman with a smile, "I really can't say. All our family records were lost in the flood."

"What happened at the restaurant when they found out you forgot your wallet?"

"The waiter kicked me out a side exit."

"What did you do?"

"I told him I belonged to a very important family, so he apologized, invited me back in, and then kicked me out the front door."

Animals

Visiting a pet shop, Bill was amazed by a bird that spoke fluently in eight languages. Paying a hefty sum for the bird, he asked to have it delivered to his house. When he got home he asked his wife if it had arrived.

"Yes," she replied. "It's in the oven for dinner."

"In the oven!" Bill shouted. "That bird can speak eight languages!"

"Then why didn't it say something?" his wife retorted.

Mama skunk was worried because she never could keep track of her two children, In and Out. Whenever In was in, Out was out, and if Out was in, In was out. One day she called Out in to her and told him to go out and bring In in. So Out went out and in no time at all he brought In in.

"Wonderful!" said Mama Skunk. "How did you find In in so short a time?"

"Easy," said Out. "In stinct."

Artists

Artist: Whatever success I have had, I owe it all to the telephone.

Friend: Why is that?

Artist: Because every time someone put me on hold, I practiced drawing on a pad.

Struggling artist: Someday people will look up at this studio and say, "Cobalt, the artist, used to paint there."

Landlord: If you don't pay me the rent tonight, they'll be saying that tomorrow.

Automobiles

The decrepit old car drove up to the toll bridge. "Fifty cents," said the toll keeper.

"Sold!" said the driver.

Baldness

Customer: Does a man with as little hair as I've got have to pay full price to have it cut?

Barber: Yes, and sometimes more. We usually charge double when we have to hunt for the hair.

Small boy in barber's chair: I want my hair cut like my daddy's—with a hole in the middle.

Children

Small Bobby had been to a birthday party. Knowing his weakness, his mother looked him straight in the eye and said, "I hope you didn't ask for a second piece of cake."

"No," replied Bobby. "I just asked Mrs. Smith for the recipe so you could make it, and she gave me two more pieces!"

Five-year-old William lived in a very strict home that didn't allow play on Sunday. One Sunday morning his mother found him sailing his toy boat in the bathtub. "William," she said, "don't you know it's wicked to sail boats on Sunday?"

"Don't worry, Mother," William responded calmly. "This isn't a pleasure trip. This is a missionary boat going to Africa."

Seven-year-old Ellen was punished one night by being made to eat her dinner alone at a little table in the corner of the dining room. The rest of the family ignored her until they heard her pray, "Thank You, Lord, for preparing a table before me in the presence of my enemies."

Little Bobby was picking up his toys, which he had scattered around the room. The visiting pastor was impressed. "Did your mother promise you something for picking them up?" he asked.

"No," Bobby replied, "but she promised me something if I didn't."

After an earthquake in California, a family sent their particularly active boy to an uncle in Arizona as they sorted through the damage. After a week, they received an e-mail from the uncle: "I'm returning Randy on the 5:45 train tonight. Send earthquake."

A man in a supermarket was pushing a cart with a screaming baby inside. As he proceeded along the aisles, he kept repeating, "Keep calm, George. Don't get excited, George. Don't yell, George."

A lady saw him and said, "You are certainly to be commended for your patience in trying to quiet little George."

"Lady," the father retorted, "*I'm* George!"

A mother called her son Prescription because it cost so much to get him filled.

A little girl stood before her mother one day, the picture of guilt and dejection. "Mother," she said, "you know the priceless vase that has been handed down in our family from generation to generation? Well, this generation just dropped it."

A father was scolding his son for not doing his homework. "When Abraham Lincoln was your age, he walked ten miles to school every day and then studied by firelight in his log cabin."

"So what?" the boy replied. "When John Kennedy was your age, he was president."

A single man berated the mothers in his neighborhood for being so hard on their children. "You need to love them," he often told them.

One day, he poured a new cement driveway. Before the cement was dry, one of the neighbor boys walked through it, and the man yelled at him.

"I thought you loved kids," a mother said.

"I love them in the abstract," the man replied, "but not in the concrete."

Mama Gnu was waiting for Papa Gnu to come home from work. "Our little boy was very bad today," she said. "I want you to punish him."

"No," said Papa Gnu, "you have to paddle your own gnu."

"What have you been doing this morning?" the mother asked her young son.

"I've been playing postman," he replied.

"How could you? You don't have any letters to deliver."

"Yes I do," the boy said, smiling. "I found a whole packet up in the attic tied up with a string, and I put one in every mailbox on our block."

Robert brought his report card home and showed it to his mother. "What's the trouble?" she asked. "Why were your grades so good the first term and so poor this time?"

"Well, you know how it is," the son replied. "They mark everything down after the holidays."

One rainy day a kindergarten teacher struggled to put on little Johnny's galoshes. Finally they were on.

"Thank you, Teacher," said Johnny, "but you know these aren't mine."

Groaning, the teacher sat Johnny down again and pulled and pulled and pulled until the galoshes came off.

Johnny continued, "They belong to my brother, but my mother made me wear them today."

In Seattle a lady was getting on a bus with several children. "My, my," said the driver. "Is this all one family, or is this a picnic?"

The woman glared at him and replied, "This is all one family, and I'll have you know, it's no picnic!"

Tommy: Grandma, if I was invited out to dinner, should I eat pie with a fork?

Grandma: Yes, indeed, Tommy.

Tommy: You don't have one here that I could practice on, do you?

"Moses had indigestion like you do," Bobby told his mother at the dinner table one Sunday.

"What makes you think that?" his mother asked.

"Well," Bobby said, "our Sunday school teacher said that when he went up on the mountain, God gave him two tablets."

Little Mary was visiting her grandmother in the country. Walking in the garden, she saw her very first peacock. Running into the house, she cried, "Oh, Grandma, come and see! One of your chickens is in bloom!"

A small boy had been in trouble all day. In the morning he hit a ball through a neighbor's window. At lunch he quarreled with his little sister and made her cry. That afternoon he teased the dog. Exasperated, his mother sent him to his room, "And ask God to make you a better boy," she instructed.

As he knelt by his bed, his mother was astounded to hear him say, "Dear God, please make me a better boy if You can. But if You can't, never mind because I'm having a pretty good time like I am."

A little boy ended his prayer earnestly. "And please, God, can't You put the vitamins in pie and cake instead of in cod-liver oil and spinach?"

A man had just come in from a long afternoon of golf. His wife kissed him and remarked that their son had just come in too. "He says he's been caddying for you," she told him.

"He has?" was his surprise. "No wonder that kid looked so familiar."

A soldier fighting in WWII received a telegram from his wife: "Gave birth to little girl this morning, both doing well."

On the envelope carrying the message was this sticker: "When you want a boy, call Western Union."

Church

At a county fair, a strong man squeezed a lemon until the last drop of juice had been removed. "I'll give $100 to anyone who can squeeze one more drop of juice from this lemon," he said.

Several husky men tried but failed. Then a scrawny individual came up, squeezed the lemon, and juice poured out.

"Remarkable!" said the strong man. "How did you do that?"

"Simple," the man replied. "I'm a church treasurer."

Five-year-old Betty was taken to church for the first time. After the service, the preacher asked her how she liked it.

"I liked the music okay," said Betty," but the commercial was too long."

Bartimaeus met another man who had been healed by Jesus, and they had a little praise meeting. The second man asked Bartimaeus, "Did the Lord take a little mud and put it on your eyes and say, 'Now see'?"

"No," replied Bartimaeus. "He simply said, 'Receive your sight.'"

"Well then," the second man said, "if He didn't put mud on your eyes, you're still blind as a bat because that's the way He healed me." The argument waxed hot, the praise meeting broke up, and the two friends parted to start two of the first sects to divide the church—the Mudites and the Antimudites.

Preacher: Let the church walk.
Deacon: Amen, let it walk.
Preacher: Let the church run.
Deacon: Amen, Preacher, let it run.
Preacher: Let the church fly.
Deacon: Amen, Brother, let it fly.
Preacher: Brethren, it'll take money to let it fly.
Deacon: Let it walk, Preacher, let it walk!

A man had visited church after church, trying to find one he liked. Finally he walked into a service just as the congregation was reading in unison, "We have done those things we should not have done and have left undone the things we should have done."

The man dropped into a pew with a sigh of relief. "Thank goodness," he said. "I've found my crowd at last."

Oil was found on the property of a church with only 40 members. As the money began to roll in, the little congregation held a special meeting to decide what to do with the money. One deacon spoke up, "I move we divide this money among the 40 members—and further, I move that no new members be taken in."

Sally: I understand that you have a very small congregation at your church.

Jane: We sure do. Whenever the preacher says, "Dearly beloved," you feel as if you've received a proposal.

Company

I was filled with annoyance and sorrow;
I could scarcely conceal my dismay.
Our guests will be leaving tomorrow.
I had hoped they'd be leaving today.

A family had company for dinner on a hot summer day. Just before the meal, the mother asked their little boy to pray.

"I don't know what to say," he said.

"Just say what I'd say if I were praying," she told him.

The boy bowed his head and said, "O Lord, why did I invite these people over on such a hot day?"

The family was seated around the dinner table with a guest, who happened to be the husband's boss.

"This is roast beef," the five-year-old son said, puzzled.

"That's right," said his mother. "Why?"

"Dad said this morning he was going to bring home a big fish for dinner tonight."

The embarrassed hostess said to her company, "I'm so sorry...I thought I told you to come over *after* dinner."

"You did," the guests replied. "And that's what we came after."

Courtesy

Two friends were seated on a bus when one noticed that the other had his eyes closed. "What's the matter, Mike?" he asked. "Don't you feel well?"

"Oh, I feel fine," Mike replied. "I just hate to see women standing."

A gentleman entered an elevator and forgot to take off his hat. The only other passenger in the elevator was a rather fussy middle-aged woman, and she asked, "Don't you take off your hat in the presence of ladies?"

"Only in the presence of old ones, ma'am," the man replied with a bow.

Two women boarded a crowded bus. One said to the other, "I wish that good-looking man would give me his seat."

Five men immediately stood up.

Crime

A lady who was going to be out for the day left a note for the milkman. "We're all gone. Don't leave anything."

When she returned, she found her house ransacked and her possessions gone. She also found a PS added to her note: "Thanks! We didn't leave much."

A prisoner was complaining about the magazines the guard brought him to read. "Nothing but stories that are 'to be continued'—and I'm being hung next Tuesday."

Judge: Why did you break into the same dress shop four times?

Prisoner: The first time, I got a dress for my wife. She made me exchange it three times.

A man was robbed, gagged, and bound to a tree. Another man walked by and found him. As soon as the gag was removed, the first man said, "They took everything but my watch."

"Can you move?" the passerby asked.

"Not a bit," the first man replied.

"Well then, give me your watch!"

Two burglars had broken into a clothing store and were busy sorting out some suits when one of them saw one marked $299. "Look at the price of this suit," he said to his partner. "Why, it's down-right robbery!"

Visitor: You poor man—what are you locked up for?

Prisoner: I suppose they think I'd get out if I weren't.

Prison warden: I've had charge of this prison for ten years. We're going to celebrate. What kind of a party do you boys suggest?

Prisoners: Open house!

A man rushed up to another man waiting for a bus. "Excuse me, sir, have you seen a policeman anywhere around here?"

"I'm sorry, I haven't seen a sign of one."

"All right, then give me your watch and your wallet."

A young couple received many valuable wedding presents and unpacked them in their new home. Shortly after, they received two tickets to a popular show in the city with a note that read, "Guess who sent these?"

The couple couldn't figure out who the tickets came from, but they decided to make good use of them. They attended the theater and had a delightful time. When they returned home, they found the house stripped of every article of value.

On the bare table in the dining room, a note with the same handwriting read, "Now you know!"

Six housewives living in the same apartment building fell into such an argument that they eventually went to court. When their case was called, they all rushed to the bench and started complaining at the same time.

The judge sat stunned as the charges and counter-charges filled the air. Suddenly he rapped for order. When the room was quiet, he calmly said, "Now then, I'll hear the oldest first."

Case closed.

A visitor at a state prison asked a prisoner, "What's your name?"

"9742," the prisoner replied.

"Is that your real name?"

"Naw, it's my pen name."

Judge: Tell me, why did you steal that lady's purse?

Burglar: Well, Your Honor, I wasn't feeling well, and I thought the change would do me good.

Police arrested a burglar, but because he was deaf, they let him go free. They couldn't convict a man without a hearing.

A counterfeiter made a mistake and turned out a number of $15 bills. Not wanting to throw them away, he decided to pass them off on a neighbor who wasn't too smart. "Say, friend," he asked, "can you give me change for a $15?"

"Sure," the neighbor replied, handing him two $6s and a $3.

A policeman patrolling a city street came upon a car in a no-parking zone with a note under the wiper. "I've circled this blocks for 20 minutes. I'm late for an appointment. If I don't park here I'll lose my job. 'Forgive us our trespasses.'"

The policeman left a parking ticket along with this note: "I've circled this block for 20 years, and if I don't give you a ticket, I'll lose my job. 'Lead us not into temptation.'"

Two judges were following each other home one night, both driving over the speed limit, and were stopped by a policeman. When their cases came up for hearing, they agreed that each should hear the other's case. The first judge went to trial, pleaded guilty, and was promptly fined $50 and costs. When they changed places, the second judge was shocked to receive a fine of $100 and costs.

"That's unfair," he said to the first. "I only fined you $50."

"I know," the first judge replied. "But there is too much of this sort of thing going on. This is the second case we've had today."

An old-timer with no knowledge of the law was elected justice of the peace. Whenever a case was brought before him, he opened his binder with a Sears-Roebuck catalog inside, thumbed through the pages, and put his finger down at random. Whatever piece of merchandise was at that spot, he would use that price as the fine.

One day a man was up for trial. Thumbing through the pages, the justice put his finger on a product and said, "You're fined $29.98."

The man began to argue, upon which his lawyer grabbed his arm and whispered, "You're just lucky he turned to Pants instead of Pianos."

A man walked past an alley on a dark night. Two thugs jumped on him, and though he put up a fierce fight, they eventually pinned him down. After they searched him, they were amazed at the small amount of change they found in his pockets. "You put up that fight for 67 cents?" one asked.

"Shucks, no," the victim replied. "I thought you were after the $500 in my shoe."

The prison warden felt sorry for one of his prisoners who never had anyone come to see him on visiting day. "Ben," he said kindly, "don't you have any friends or family?"

"Oh, sure," Ben replied, "but they're all in here."

Judge: What's your name and occupation, and what are you charged with?

Prisoner: My name is Sparks. I'm an electrician, and I'm charged with battery.

Judge: Officer, put this guy in a dry cell.

Bandit (to bank teller): Get a move on! I'm in a no-parking zone.

First Prisoner: What are you in for?

Second Prisoner: Well, I want to be a warden, so I thought I'd start at the bottom and work my way up.

Some think we could help juvenile delinquents by getting them interested in bowling. But all that would do is get them off the streets and into the alleys.

A gunman suddenly appeared at a paymaster's window of a large plant and demanded, "Never mind the payroll. Just hand over the welfare fund, the group insurance premiums, the pension fund, and the withholding taxes."

Doctors

A country doctor came out of the post office and found a group of kids gathered around his old car, making fun of it. "That's quite a beat-up rattletrap you've got," one boy said.

"Yes," the doctor replied, "but it's paid for." Then, pointing at the children, he said, "But you're not…and you're not…and you're not."

Just as a dentist was leaving his office to meet a friend for golf, the phone rang. "It's a woman with a toothache," his secretary said. "She wants to know if she can come in right away."

"Tell her I won't be available," the dentist said. "Tell her I already have an appointment to fill 18 cavities this afternoon."

A doctor's five-year-old answered the door. "Is the doctor in?" inquired the caller.

"No, sir."

"Have you any idea when he will be back?"

"I don't know, sir. He went out on an eternity case."

"Doctor," the lady said loudly, bouncing into the room. "I want to know what's wrong with me."

"Well, ma'am," he said, looking her over. "I've three things to tell you. First, you should lose at least 50 pounds. Second, cut down on your makeup. And third, I'm an artist—the doctor is on the next floor."

Education

Asked if a year in college had made any difference in his son, the farmer replied, "Well, he's still a good hand at plowing, but now instead of saying, 'Whoa, Becky! Haw and git up!' he says, 'Halt, Rebecca! Pivot and proceed!'"

A laddie at college named Breeze,
Weighed down by BAs and PhDs,
Collapsed from the strain.
Said the doctor, "It's plain
You're killing yourself by degrees."

A divinity student named Tweedle
Refused to accept his degree.
He didn't object to the "Tweedle,"
But he hated the "Tweedle, DD."

Bill: Why do you always call your mail carrier Professor?

Fred: Oh, it's an honorary title. I'm taking a correspondence course.

Tom: Why the toothbrush in your coat lapel?
Sam: It's my class pin. I go to Colgate University.

A professor marked the test so strictly that he took off points for having periods upside down.

Little Billy came home from his first day at school and told his mother he was never going back. "What's the use?" he said. "I can't read and I can't write, and the teacher won't let me talk."

Charlie was failing fifth grade, so he asked a college student to tutor him.

"I'll be glad to help you," the student replied. "I charge $12 for the first month and $6 for the second."

"Great," Charlie told him. "I'll come the second month."

A teacher told her class, "Some plants have the prefix *dog*, such as the dogwood and the dog violet. Who can name another plant prefixed by the word *dog*?"

A smart boy in the back called out and said, "How about collie flower?"

Father: Why were you kept after school?

Son: I didn't know where the Azores were.

Father: In the future, remember where you put things.

"Are your father and mother in?" asked the visitor of the small boy who answered the door.

"They was in," the boy said, "but they is out."

"They *was* in? They *is* out? Where's your grammar?"

"She's upstairs for a nap," the boy replied.

A superintendent visiting a country school was shocked at the noisy classroom. Seeing one boy taller than the rest and talking a great deal, he seized him by the collar, marched him to the next room, and stood him in the corner. "Now you stand there and be quiet," he commanded.

Ten minutes later a small head appeared round the door, and a meek voice asked, "Please, sir, may we have our teacher back?"

Tom was home from college for a visit. "May I tell you a narrative, Mom?"

The mother, not being used to his new vocabulary, said, "A narrative?"

"A narrative is a tale," Tom said.

That night when going to bed, he said, "Could you extinguish the light, Mom?" Seeing the look on her face, he added, "*Extinguish* means 'to put out.'"

A few days later, the dog scratched at the door, and the mother said, "Tom, please take the dog by the narrative and extinguish him."

Jeff: What is your brother in college?
John: A halfback.
Jeff: No, I mean in his studies.
John: Oh, in his studies he's way back.

A college student wrote his parents a letter, pressuring them for more money. "I can't understand how you call yourself a kind father," he wrote, "when you haven't sent me a check in three weeks. What sort of kindness do you call that?"

His father replied, "That is unremitting kindness."

Professor: Name two pronouns.
Student: Who, me?

First student: Great Scott! I've forgotten who wrote *Ivanhoe*.

Second student: I'll tell you if you tell me who the dickens wrote *A Tale of Two Cities*.

38

Chemistry professor: What can you tell me about nitrates?

Student: Well, I know they're cheaper than day rates.

Farming

The farmer made his chickens swim in hot water so they would lay hard-boiled eggs.

City visitor: Mr. Farmer, why are you running that steam roller over your field?

Farmer: This year I'm raising mashed potatoes.

A chicken farmer had trouble with his flock and wrote to the Department of Agriculture: "Dear sir, something is wrong with my chickens. Every morning I find two or three lying on the ground cold and stiff with their feet in the air. Can you tell me what is the matter?"

After a while he received the following letter: "Dear sir, your chickens are dead."

Food

A scientist crossed a potato with a sponge. It tastes terrible, but holds a lot of gravy.

Customer: I haven't found any ham in this sandwich yet.

Waiter: Try another bite.

Customer (taking huge mouthful): Nope, none yet.

Waiter: Doggone it! You must have gone right past it.

Customer to waitress: Those sausages you gave me were meat at one end and cornmeal at the other.

Waitress: I know. In these hard times, it's hard to make both ends meat.

Two old settlers, confirmed bachelors, sat in the backwoods. The conversation drifted around to cooking. "I got one of them cookin' books once but couldn't do nothing with it."

"Too much fancy words in it, eh?"

"No, every one of them recipes began the same way—'Take a clean dish'—and that did it."

"What's this, honey?" said the groom to his new bride, as he looked at the food on his plate.

"Devil's food cake," she replied.

"I thought you were making angel food cake," he said.

"I was, but it fell."

Grandparenting

A grandmother was so tickled to learn that her grandchildren were coming for a week that she put $10 in the offering plate. When the children went home at the end of the week, her joy must have doubled because that Sunday she put in $20.

A grandmother saw a friend in a supermarket and started to ask, "Did I tell you about the cute thing my granddaughter said—"

But her friend cut her short. "Before you start, I warn you that I demand equal time—and I have 16 grandchildren!"

Health

"Is this a healthy town?" a New Yorker asked a resident of Phoenix.

"Sure is," replied the resident. "When I first came here, I didn't have the strength to say a word, I had hardly a hair on my head, I couldn't walk across the room, and I even had to be lifted in and out of bed."

"That's wonderful!" exclaimed the tourist. "How long have you been here?"

"I was born here."

At a pre-op appointment, a surgeon told his patient, "I believe in getting my patients up and around as soon as possible. Three hours after the operation, you'll sit up. Five hours after, you'll stand up. In eight hours you'll be walking."

"Fine," the patient said. "But will you let me lie down during the operation?"

A movie star on a cruise saw a man suffering from a cold. "I'll tell you what to do," she instructed. "Go back to your room, drink a lot of orange juice, take two aspirin, and cover yourself with all the blankets you can find. I should know what I'm talking about. I'm Billie Burke of Hollywood."

The man smiled warmly and replied, "Thanks. I'm Dr. Mayo of the Mayo Clinic."

A surgeon examined a new patient most carefully. After studying the X-rays, he turned to the man and said, "Could you pay for an operation if I told you it was necessary?"

The patient thought for a moment and then replied, "Would you find one necessary if I told you I couldn't pay for it?"

"I'm so grateful for my first-aid training," said the girl. "Last night there was an accident right in front of my house. An old man was knocked down by a car and was bleeding all over. He was moaning something awful. That's when my training came in handy. I remembered to put my head between my knees to keep from fainting."

Heaven

A man died and went to heaven. Talking with St. Peter, he asked him how long a minute was in heaven.

"A million years," said St. Peter.

"Well, how much is a penny worth in heaven?"

"A million dollars," St. Peter replied.

"Wow," said the man. "Can you lend me a penny?"

"In a minute," said St. Peter.

Heroes

Larry had rescued his friend from the icy waters of a frozen lake, crawling out onto the thin ice to the spot where Grant was struggling desperately to stay afloat and pushing a board to him.

"That was certainly a heroic thing to do," a bystander commended when both boys were safe on land. "You have a lot of courage."

"It wasn't that," Larry said modestly. "He had my new skates on."

Housekeeping

Beth: One of our neighbors is so neat she puts file folders in her wastebaskets.

Ann: My neighbor puts popcorn in her pancakes so they'll flip over by themselves.

Husband: You haven't washed that frying pan in weeks.

Wife: That makes me an authority on ancient grease.

Housekeeper: There are six men here with vacuums. They all have appointments to give demonstrations.

Employer: Yes, I sent for them. Put them all in different rooms and tell them to get busy.

Insurance

Two vacationing business owners were comparing notes on a Miami beach. One said, "I'm here on the insurance money I collected—got $50,000 for fire damage."

"Me too," the second merchant said, "but I got $100,000 for a flood."

After a long silence, the first man said, "Tell me, how do you start a flood?"

A man asked his agent about buying life insurance.

"Do you drive a car?" asked the agent.

"No," replied the man.

"Do you ride in buses or taxis?"

"No."

"Do you fly much?"

"No."

"I'm sorry," the agent said firmly, "but we don't insure pedestrians."

A man had just insured his property against fire. "What would I get if this building should burn down tonight?" he asked his agent.

"I'd say about ten years," the agent replied.

Love

The young engineer took his girlfriend in his arms and said, "Darling, I love you. I may not be rich like Henry, I may not have a yacht or limousine like he does, and I don't live in a fancy house like his, but I would do anything for you."

"You would?" the girlfriend replied. "Well, how about introducing me to Henry?"

"Use a word ten times, and it will be yours for life," the English teacher told his class.

In the back of the room, a pert blonde closed her eyes and chanted under her breath, "Kurt, Kurt, Kurt…"

Q: What did the wedding guests say when an X-ray technician married one of her former patients?

A: I wonder what she saw in him.

They met in a revolving door and have been going around together ever since.

Girl: My boyfriend makes me so nervous, I'm losing weight.

Friend: Are you going to break up with him?

Girl: As soon as I lose 15 more pounds.

Gladys: Listen to what my boyfriend says about me in his letter: "Darling, I think of you all day long—your naturally wavy hair, your brownish-gray eyes, your slightly prominent cheekbones, your 24-inch waist…"

Mabel: That's a strange love letter.

Gladys: Oh, didn't you know? Bob writes descriptions of missing people for the police department.

"It was a lousy date," the fellow said. "She disagreed with my bumper sticker and I disagreed with her T-shirt."

"Dear Alice," wrote the young man. "I remember proposing to you last night, but I forgot whether you said yes or no."

"Dear Bob," Alice wrote back. "So glad you wrote. I knew I said no to someone last night, but I had forgotten who it was."

One man spent so much money on a girl during their two-year courtship that he finally married her for his money.

Arthur and Mary were seated on a park bench. "I wish I were an octopus," Arthur sighed.

"Whatever for?" asked Mary.

"Because I would have eight arms to hold you with."

There was a long silence, and then Mary said, "Why don't you use the two you have?"

Minister's daughter to boyfriend: Dad's sermon tonight is on the text "Love one another." Don't you want to go?

Boyfriend: Well, I'd much rather stay here and practice what he's preaching.

He: If you'll give me your telephone number, I'll call you sometime.

She: It's in the book.

He: Fine! And what's your name?

She: That's in the book too.

"Tell me all about it," a man said to a friend who was worrying. "Get it off your chest."

"I wish I could," the friend moaned. "I've got the name Maggie tattooed there, and I'm engaged to marry Judy."

"You want to marry me?" the girl asked in surprise. "You've only known me three months."

"Oh, I've known you longer than that," the young man replied. "I've worked two years in the bank where your father has his account."

He: The first time you contradict me, I'm going to kiss you.

She: No, you're not.

"Why did you break your engagement to Tom?"

"He deceived me. He said he was a liver and kidney specialist, but he only works in a butcher shop."

She: Do you love me, dear?

He: Yes, sweetheart.

She: Would you die for me?

He: No, mine is an undying love.

Father: What income do you have to support my daughter?

Boyfriend: $20,000 a year.

Father: I see, then with her annual income of $20,000 from me—

Boyfriend: That's what I'm counting.

Marooned

A group of people was shipwrecked on a desert island. After many months, a passing ship saw their plight and sent a smaller boat ashore. One of the sailors threw a bundle of newspapers on the beach and shouted, "The captain wants to know if you still want to be rescued after you've read the news."

Marriage

A man went to a stationery store to purchase a pen and pencil set. "I'm buying this for my wife," he said.

"Is it a surprise?" the salesclerk asked.

"I'll say so," the husband replied. "She's expecting a car."

Two girls were talking about a third girl. "She's only 25," the first girl said, "but she's been married three times. And all three husbands were named William."

"You don't say!" replied the second. "She's a regular Bill collector."

A man came home from work one day to find his house a shambles. The beds weren't made, the sink was filled with dirty dishes, clothes and toys and books were all over the floor, and dinner wasn't ready. "What in the world happened?" he asked his wife.

"Nothing," she said. "You always ask me what I do all day. Well, take a look. Today I didn't do it."

An usher brought word to a pastor that a young couple had come in during the morning service and wished to be married. The pastor sent word back that he would conduct the ceremony immediately after the morning service.

When the time came, he announced that there was a young man and a young woman here who wanted to be married. "If they will come forward, I will be most happy to perform the ceremony." Nine women and five men hurried to the front of the sanctuary.

"I don't think you should marry Henry," a mother told her daughter. "He's a dentist and you're a manicurist."

"What does that have to do with it?"

"Well, you'll just fight tooth and nail."

"I've decided on a name for the baby," the new mother said. "I'll call her Matilda."

Her husband didn't care too much for the selection, but he decided to choose his words carefully. "That's great," he said cheerfully. "The first girl I ever loved was named Matilda, and the name will bring back pleasant memories."

After a brief period of silence, his wife said, "How about Elizabeth?"

She's my wife due to the fact that the Lonely Hearts Club lied about their free ten-day trial and exchange plan.

"O Lord," the unmarried woman prayed fervently, "I'm not asking for anything for myself. But please, couldn't You send my mother a son-in-law?"

"Of course you can buy the hat," a husband told his wife. "I like that middle-aged look it gives you."

Husband: Before we got married, you said you were well off.

Wife: I was, and I didn't know it.

There's nothin' like a weddin'
To make a feller learn;
At first he thinks she's his'n,
But later finds he's her'n.

Comedians make light of marriage, but it has been proven that married life is healthy. Statistics show that single people die sooner than married folks. So if you're looking for a long life and a slow death, get married.

She didn't want to marry him for his money, but couldn't figure out any other way to get it.

A 70-year-old millionaire fell in love with a sweet little 23-year-old and was considering proposing. He asked a longtime friend, "Do you think I'd have a better chance if I told her I was 60 instead of 70?"

"Your best bet is to tell her you're 80," his friend replied.

Little Marjorie attended a fashionable wedding. Afterward she said, "I can't make out who she married. She walked up the aisle with an old man and came back down with a younger one."

"Mr. Jones," began the timid young man, "er...uh...that is, can...er...I...will you..."

"Yes, my boy, you may have her," said the girl's father.

"What's that? Have whom?" he gasped.

"My daughter, of course," the father replied. "You want to marry her, don't you?"

"Why, no," said the young man. "I just wanted to know if you could lend me $25."

"Certainly not!" the father answered sharply. "I hardly know you!"

A man looked unusually pensive. "A penny for your thoughts," his wife said.

"I was wondering what epitaph I should put on your tombstone," he replied.

His spouse, who was in perfect health, resented this remark. "Oh, that's simple," she responded. "Just put, 'Wife of the Above.'"

Memory

I remember, I remember
Incidents of days long gone;
I recapture every moment
As I ramble on and on.
But my tales would be more pleasing
And I'd never be a bore,
If I only could remember
Whom I told them to before.

      —Paul Tullen

The absentminded professor staggered from a train, his complexion pale. "I rode backward for ten hours," he told his friend. "I never could stand that."

"Why didn't you ask the person sitting across from you to change seats?" the friend asked.

"I couldn't," the professor replied. "No one was sitting there."

Absentminded professor: Lady, what are you doing in my bed?

61

Lady: I like this neighborhood, I like this house, I like this room, and I like this bed. Besides, I'm your wife!

Absentminded professor: I forgot to take my umbrella this morning.

Wife: When did you miss it?

Professor: When I reached up to close it after the rain had stopped.

Absentminded professor: Why is there a vase of flowers on the table today?

Wife: Why, today is your wedding anniversary.

Professor: Indeed! Well, well, let me know when yours is so I can do the same for you.

"Mr. Perkins left his umbrella again. I do believe he'd lose his head if it were loose."

"You're probably right. Only yesterday I heard him say he was going to Colorado for his lungs."

Military

The draftee was awakened roughly by his platoon sergeant after the rookie's first night in the army barracks. "It's four thirty," roared the sergeant.

"Four thirty!" gasped the recruit. "Man, you better get to bed. We've got a big day tomorrow."

A soldier, serving in the desert, was complaining about the soup. "If you'd put the lid on tighter, we wouldn't get so much dust in it," he said to the cook.

"See here," said the cook angrily. "Your business is to serve your country."

"Serve it, yes," the soldier replied. "Not eat it."

Corporal: Do you know that ugly sap of an officer standing over there? He's the meanest egg I've ever seen.

Young woman: Do you know who I am? I'm that officer's daughter.

Corporal: Do you know who I am?

Young woman: No.

Corporal: Thank goodness!

A soldier leaving an Army base was overheard saying to a buddy, "This has got to be love at first sight. I'm on an eight-hour pass."

Then there was the private who saluted the refrigerator in the mess hall because it was General Electric.

"No," growled the sergeant. "You can't have a new pair of shoes. The pair you're wearing aren't worn out."

"Aren't worn out?" said the recruit. "Why, if I step on a dime, I can tell whether it's heads or tails!"

Ministers

A hip kid attended church. After the service he told the minister, "Man, I really dug that sermon."

"I don't understand."

"Dad, your talk was cool—it was gone, man."

The pastor was shaken. "I still don't understand what you're saying."

"What I mean is, I really went for what you said. In fact, I put a hundred-dollar bill in the plate."

The pastor replied, "Crazy, man, crazy!"

A minister was preaching his farewell sermon, and all during the service an elderly saint was in tears. At the door the pastor said to her, "Don't cry, Sister, the conference will send you a better preacher."

"That's what they said the last time," she sobbed.

A millionaire lay dying. He had never gone to church, but at the last hour he called in a minister to whom he weakly muttered, "If I leave $100,000 or so to the church, will that help me get into heaven?"

"Well," the minister cautiously answered, "I couldn't say for sure, but it's worth a try."

One minister had horrible handwriting. A parishioner invited him to dinner and received a reply so hopelessly scrawled, she couldn't tell whether he had accepted.

"Take it to the pharmacist," her husband replied. "They can read handwriting no matter how bad it is."

The lady did so. After looking at the note for a few minutes, the pharmacist took it to the back of the store, came back a few minutes later with a bottle of pills, and said to the lady, "That'll be $20."

After a fund-raiser at church one Sunday morning, the preacher's wife found her daughter out in the henhouse. She had several hens cornered and was saying, "Every one of you hens that'll promise to lay an egg today, hold up your hand."

The ministers of a particular denomination were attending a conference in a large Midwestern city. On the third day a taxi driver commented, "These people came to town with a ten-dollar bill and the Ten Commandments, and they haven't broken either of them yet."

"Please go easy on the bill for repairing my car," the minister told the mechanic. "Remember, I am a poor preacher."

"I know," replied the mechanic. "I heard you last Sunday."

A minister was making a pastoral call. Just before he left, he said he wished to read the Bible and have prayer. The father turned to one of his children and sanctimoniously said, "Go bring that book your father is always reading." Soon, to the minister's delight and the father's embarrassment, the son returned with the swimsuit issue of *Sports Illustrated*.

First minister: How many people attend your church?

Second minister: Eight hundred.

First minister: But I thought your church seated only 400 people.

Second minister: That's true, but my people are so narrow, they can sit two in a seat.

A minister awoke one night and saw a burglar going through his dresser drawers. "What are you doing?" asked the minister.

"I'm looking for money."

"Wait a minute," the minister said as he jumped out of bed. "I'll look with you."

A minister had a ready Scripture for every occasion. While he was preaching, he accidentally swallowed a fly and quickly said, "He was a stranger, and I took him in."

The minister had received several negative votes on his last recall. His little girl had overheard who voted them, but the father told her not to tell him.

The next Sunday, she was seated on the front row at a baptismal service. As the minister prepared to immerse the first lady, the little girl shouted, "No, no, Daddy, she wasn't one of them!"

The minister asked for prayer requests. "I'm having trouble managing my money," Brother Brown replied. "I throw it around—I'm too generous."

"We'll pray for Brother Brown," the preacher replied. "But first, let's take the offering."

Two deacons were having a little chat about their pastor's strong points and weak points. "I think what our pastor needs to do," said one of them, "is to get more fire into his sermons."

The other disagreed. "I think he needs to get more of his sermons into the fire."

"We need a chandelier," the pastor said in the board meeting.

"I'm against it," a miserly member replied.

"Why?" the pastor asked.

"First, nobody can spell it. Second, nobody in the church can play it. And third, what this church needs more than a chandelier is more light."

There were two brothers—one a baseball pitcher and the other a minister. One day they were discussing their salaries.

"I don't understand, Bill," the preacher said. "I spent four years in college and three years in seminary, and I only get $35,000 a year. You've never done anything but play ball, and you get $200,000 a year. What's up with that?"

His brother thought a minute and then said, "It's all in the delivery."

A minister phoned long-distance to a clergy friend in another state. "Do you want this station-to-station?" asked the operator.

"No," he replied, "make it parson-to-parson."

A minister was about to baptize a baby. "What's the baby's name?" he asked the father.

"William Patrick Arthur Timothy John MacArthur," the father replied.

Turning to his assistant, the preacher said, "A little more water please."

A minister passing along the street noticed a group of boys gathered around a dog. "What's up?" the preacher asked with a friendly smile.

"We're swapping lies," said one of the boys. "Whoever tells the biggest one gets the dog."

"Boys! I'm shocked," said the preacher. "When I was a boy your age, I never told a lie."

"You win!" chorused the boys. "The dog's yours."

Two preachers were having lunch at a farm. The farmer's wife had cooked a couple of chickens. Later the farmer was conducting his guests around the farm, when an old rooster began to crow.

"Sounds mighty proud of himself," one of the guests said.

"No wonder," said the farmer. "He's got two sons in the ministry."

Money

Jones: How do you spend your money?

Smith: Thirty percent for shelter, 30 percent for clothing, 40 percent for food, and 20 percent for amusement.

Jones: But that adds up to 120 percent.

Smith: Don't I know it!

Sandy joined a golf club and was told by the professional that if his name was on his golf balls and they were lost, they would be returned to him when found.

"Good. Put my name on the ball, and could you also put MD after it? I'm a doctor."

The pro agreed.

"One more thing," Sandy said. "Could you squeeze 'Hours 10 to 3' on it as well?"

When the young lady broke up with the doctor, he not only asked for all his presents back but also sent her a bill for 47 visits.

A party of tourists were enjoying the Grand Canyon. "I wonder what made this gorge?" one tourist asked.

"Well," the guide replied, "it's said that a miser once owned a ranch near here, and one day he lost a golf ball down a gopher hole."

Bookkeeper: I'll have to have a raise, sir. Three other companies are after me.

Employer: Really? What companies?

Bookkeeper: Light, phone, and gas.

An elderly man put a dollar in the Salvation Army drum. Then he asked the bell ringer, "What do you do with the money?"

"Give it to the Lord," she answered.

"How old are you?"

"Nineteen," the bell ringer replied.

"I'm 87," the old man replied, taking his dollar from the drum. "You don't need to bother. I'll likely see the Lord before you will."

The expectant father was a little on the broke side, so he took his wife to the Pizza Palace to have her baby because he heard it had free delivery.

The sons of a lawyer, a doctor, and a minister were bragging about how much money their fathers made.

"My father comes home from court with as much as a thousand dollars," the lawyer's son said.

"My father earns up to two thousand dollars for an operation," the doctor's son retorted.

"That's nothing," the minister's son said. "My father preaches for only 20 minutes on Sunday morning, and it takes four men to carry the money."

A pastor asked all to stand who would be willing to pledge to the building fund. "But first," he said, "will the organist please play 'The Star Spangled Banner'?"

Walking along a street, a man heard frightened screams from a house. Rushing in, he found a mother frantic because her little son had swallowed a quarter. Seizing the child by the heels, he held him up and gave him a few shakes, and the coin dropped to the floor.

The mother thanked him, asking, "Are you a doctor? You certainly knew how to get that money out of him."

"No," the man replied, "I'm from the Internal Revenue Service."

The husband was so cheap, he hung 50 state pennants on the wall instead of taking his wife on a vacation.

"How do you manage to have so much money all the time?"

"It's simple. I never pay old debts."

"But how about the new ones?"

"I let them grow old."

One bridegroom was so miserly that he went to Niagara Falls alone on his honeymoon because his bride had already been there.

"You pay a small deposit," said the salesman, "and then make no more payments for six months."

"Who told you about us?" demanded the customer.

The bill collector reminded Joe he was three payments behind on his piano.

"Well," replied Joe, "the company advertises, 'Pay as you play,' and I play very poorly."

The salesman was trying to sell a family a freezer. "You'll save enough on your food bill to pay for it," he said.

"I can understand that," the husband said, "but we're paying for our car on the bus fare we save, paying for our washing machine on the laundry money we save, and our house on the rent we save. Right now our monthly payments are so high, we just can't afford to save any more money."

"Dear Mom and Dad," the college student wrote, "I'm so worried about you. I haven't heard from you in over a month. Please send me a check so I'll know that everything is all right at home."

A miser taking a train trip got off at every stop and went into the depot. A fellow traveler asked him the reason for his strange behavior.

"I have heart trouble," the miser explained. "My doctor said I may drop dead any minute, so I just buy a ticket from station to station."

Hubby: The bank has returned our check.

Wife: Splendid! What can we buy with it this time?

A tightwad made his wife keep an account of her cash. Each week he went over it, grumbling. One evening he complained, "Look here, Sarah, three teeth extracted, $200; medication, $40. That's $240 in one week for your own private pleasure. Do you think I'm made of money?"

Music

A lady who had been taking music lessons was nervously singing her first solo in church. She came to the phrase, "the fairest of ten thousand," and her voice broke on the word "ten." She tried a second time and failed. "Give me my note again," she told the organist, and she made the third attempt in vain.

Then came a voice from the audience: "Why don't you start over and try for *five* thousand?"

Someone told a singer he had a mellow voice. He went home and looked up the word "mellow" in the dictionary and found that it meant "overripe and almost rotten."

A musician was practicing his sax in the wee small hours of the morning when the landlord knocked on the door. "Do you know there's a little old lady sick upstairs?" he asked.

"No," the musician replied, "but if you'll hum a few bars, I'll give it a try."

The egotistical singer asked the critic, "Did you notice how my voice filled the hall tonight?"

"Yes," the critic answered. "And I saw several people leaving to make room for it."

An eccentric cello player sawed away on one note hour after hour and day after day. Someone asked him why he didn't play other notes as other players did.

He answered, "They're hunting for it. I've found it."

Mother: What do you think of Junior's piano playing?

Father: Well, he does use the biblical method.

Mother: What, "Seek and you will find"?

Father: No, he doesn't let his left hand know what his right hand is doing.

Two music editors were looking over a new manuscript. "I've never heard such corny lyrics, such simpering sentimentality, such repetitious, uninspired melody," one said. "Man, we've got a hit on our hands!"

Daughter (listening to her favorite new CD): Did you ever hear anything like this?

Father: Can't say I have, although I once heard a truck filled with milk cans crash into a truck filled with ducks. That sounded similar.

Politicians

"How dare you insult me in your paper!" roared the politician. "I demand a public apology."

"Just a moment," answered the editor. "We printed the item exactly as you gave it to us—that you had resigned your office."

"That's not the point," the politician replied. "Why did you put it in the column under 'Public Improvements'?"

A surgeon, an architect, and a politician were arguing as to whose profession was the oldest. The surgeon said, "Eve was made from Adam's rib, and that surely was a surgical operation."

"Maybe," said the architect, "but before that, order was created out of chaos, and that was an architectural job."

"Perhaps," the politician said. "But somebody created the chaos first."

Prayer

Two men were adrift in a lifeboat with little hope of being rescued. Finally one of them began to pray. "O Lord, I've broken most of Your commandments, but if You will spare my life now, I promise You—"

"Wait a minute," said his friend. "Don't promise too much. I think I see a boat in the distance."

As a boat was sinking, the captain asked, "Does anybody know how to pray?"

"Yes," one man spoke confidently. "I do, Captain."

"Okay then," the captain replied, "you go ahead and pray. The rest of us will put on life jackets. We're one short."

Psychiatry

"Please help me, Doctor," the patient said to the psychiatrist. "I have this terrible feeling that I'm a dog."

"How long have you felt like that?" the psychiatrist asked.

"Ever since I was a puppy," the patient replied.

A patient was informed by his psychiatrist that he could consider himself cured of his delusion that he was Napoleon.

"Oh, wonderful!" cried the happy man. "Where's the phone? I must call Josephine and tell her the great news."

A woman went to a psychiatrist and said, "Doctor, I want to talk to you about my husband. He thinks he's a refrigerator."

"That seems harmless," said the doctor.

"Maybe so," the woman said. "But he sleeps with his mouth open, and the light keeps me awake."

Real Estate

What a sad tale about the two-story house—the Realtor told the buyer one story before he bought it and another one afterward.

Sports

"I'd move heaven and earth to be able to break 100 on this golf course," sighed Mac.

"Try heaven," advised his caddie. "You've already moved most of the earth."

"Why don't you play golf with George anymore?" Pete's wife asked.

"Would you play with someone who puts down the wrong score and moves the ball when you aren't watching?" asked Pete.

"No," his wife replied, "I certainly wouldn't."

"Neither will George."

The red ants and black ants were playing baseball, and the score was tied in the ninth inning. A black ant got up to bat and hit the ball out in the corner of right field. He ran to first base, to second, and to third while the black ants screamed and cheered. Suddenly, when he was almost to home, an elephant came along, stepped on the black ant, and killed him.

All the black ants came running over to him and cried, "Why did you step on our black ant?"

"I didn't mean to kill him," the elephant cried with big elephant tears. "I only meant to trip him."

Sunday School

A Sunday school teacher tried her best to get her lesson across, but it was spring, and the students' attention was on the baseball game they were playing after church. In summing up the lesson, she asked the class, "Boys, who defeated the Philistines?"

One of them replied, "I don't know, Mrs. Brown. They're not in our league. But the Dodgers beat the Braves in a doubleheader yesterday."

The Sunday school teacher had on a beautiful new dress, and her students immediately noticed it. Mary Jane sat quietly for a while and then said, "I suppose it cost an awful lot. But we've been bringing you money every Sunday morning, so I guess you could afford it."

"This morning," said the teacher, "we'll learn about Ruth the gleaner. Who can tell me anything about Ruth?" A small boy raised his hand.

"Well, Willie, what do you know about Ruth?" the teacher asked.

"I know he gleaned 60 home runs one season."

Taxes

The months in which we feel free from tax worries are those with an *X* in their names.

Father to mother: I can't bawl out Junior. Every time I do, he reminds me he's an exemption on my income tax.

Teenagers

"Doctor," said the man, "I'm in an awful state. Whenever the phone rings I almost jump out of my skin. The doorbell gives me the willies. If I see a stranger at the door, I start shaking. I'm even afraid to look at a newspaper. What's come over me, anyway?"

The doctor patted him on the back. "There, there. I know what you're going through. My teenage daughter just got her driver's license too."

A father said to his lazy teenage son, "Why don't you get a job?"

"Why?"

"Well, you could earn a lot of money."

"Why?"

"If you worked hard and saved your money, you'd have a bank account. Wouldn't you like that?"

"Why?"

"I'll tell you," shouted the father. "With a bank account you could retire, and then you wouldn't have to work anymore."

"I'm not working now," retorted the son.

Texans

A wealthy Texas oilman tried to cash a huge personal check, but it came back from the bank with Insufficient Funds stamped on it. Beneath the stamped words was the handwritten notation, "Not you—us."

The Texan was bragging about all the heroes of the Alamo. A man from Boston, not to be outdone, began boasting of Paul Revere.

"Paul Revere?" the Texan said. "Wasn't he the man who had to ride for help?"

Tourists

A tourist paid a farmer ten dollars to pull him out of a rut in an especially muddy road. "Do many other people get stuck on this road?" he asked.

"Oh yes," said the farmer. "Sometimes we pull out ten or twelve a day."

"Do you pull them out at night too?"

"Oh no," replied the farmer. "At night we haul water for the roads."

Tourist: This is a dangerous precipice. Why doesn't the city put up a warning sign?

Guide: They had a warning sign here for two years, but no one fell over, so they took it down.

A tourist traveling through Texas got into a conversation with an old settler and his son at a filling station. "Looks as though we might have rain," said the tourist.

"I hope so," replied the native. "Not so much for myself as for my boy here. I've seen it rain."

A woman traveling by train was talking with her seatmate. "I've been to San Jose," she said.

"I think it's pronounced San Ho-say," the other person said. "In California you pronounce the Js as Hs. When were you there?"

The lady hesitated and then said, "In Hune and Huly."

Hotel manager: Your room is ready, but because of a shortage of help, you'll have to make your own bed.

Guest: That's no problem.

Manager: Okay, here's a hammer and saw.

A group of American tourists were led through an ancient castle in Europe. "This place is 600 years old," the guide told them. "Nothing has been altered in all those years."

One woman whispered, "They must have the same landlord I have."

Trains

Conductor: Sorry, ma'am, but we have learned that the station where you intended to get off has been burned to the ground.

Impatient lady: That's all right. They'll probably have it rebuilt by the time this train gets there.

Railroad agent: Here's another farmer who is suing us on account of his cows.

Official: Did one of our trains hit one of his cows?

Agent: No, he claims our trains go by so slow that the passengers lean out the windows and milk the cows when they go by.

A certain train had been late every day for years, but one day it rolled into the depot exactly on time. The surprised and pleased passengers got together and took up a collection for the engineer and presented it to him with an eloquent speech.

The engineer refused the gift reluctantly, saying, "It breaks my heart to do this, as I sure do need the money, but this here is yesterday's train."

Nell: My new boyfriend is so romantic. He always calls me Fair Lady.

Belle: Force of habit, my dear. He's a streetcar conductor.

Weather

A Baptist pastor from Texas, during an extended drought, visited a pastor friend in Florida. "How are you getting along without water in your state?" the friend asked.

"Well," the pastor replied, "it's so bad that the Baptists are sprinkling, the Methodists are using a damp cloth, and the Presbyterians are taking a rain check."

A visitor to Kansas saw a man sitting by the ruins of a house that had been blown away. "Was this your house, my friend?"

"Yep."

"Any of your family blown away by the storm?"

"Yep, wife and four kids."

"Man, why aren't you out hunting for them?"

"Well, stranger, I've been in this country quite a spell. The wind's due to change this afternoon, so I figure I might as well wait here till it brings 'em back."

Arctic Explorer: It was so cold where we were, the candle froze and we couldn't blow it out.

Second Explorer: That's nothing. Where we were the words came out of our mouths in pieces of ice, and we had to fry them to see what we were talking about.

A man was complaining that the heat wasn't working in his apartment. "It's bad enough in the daytime," he said, "but at night I wake up and hear my teeth chattering on the dressing table."

Wills

A wealthy man's will was being read, and the relatives all listened expectantly, especially his playboy nephew. Finally the lawyer read, "And to my nephew Charlie, whom I promised to remember in my will, Hi there, Charlie!"

The family gathered around as the lawyer read the will of their wealthy family member. "To my dear wife," the lawyer read, "I leave my house, 50 acres of land, and $1 million. To my son, Sam, I leave my two cars and $100,000. To my daughter, Bessie, I leave my yacht and $100,000. And to my brother-in-law, who always insisted that health is better than wealth, I leave my sunlamp."

"Why are you so sad?" a friend asked a man whose aunt had just died. "You never appeared to care much for the poor old lady."

"I didn't," admitted the man. "But I was responsible for keeping her in the mental hospital the last five years. Now she's left me all her money, and I have to prove she was of sound mind."

Women

She's so modest, she pulls down the shade to change her mind.

Work

"Who was that on the telephone?" the woman asked her new housekeeper.

"I dunno," the housekeeper answered. "Someone just said, 'Long distance from New York,' so I said, 'It certainly is,' and hung up."

Employer: For this job we want someone who is responsible.

Applicant: That's me. The last job I had, every time something went wrong, they said I was responsible.

A lady asked the manager of a shoe store, "Do you have any loafers?"

"Yes," he said, "we have several. I'll see if I can get one of them to wait on you."

Employer: Why were you late this morning?

Employee: It's because of my alarm clock. There are nine of us in the family, and the clock was only set for eight.

A printing plant didn't hire an applicant because she wasn't the type.

A customer wanted to buy a chicken, and the butcher had only one left. He weighed it and said, "A beauty. It'll be $1.25."

"That's not big enough," said the customer. The butcher went into the back room, came out with the same chicken, and put it on the scales, adding his thumb for extra weight. "This one is $1.85," he said.

"That's fine," the customer said. "I'll take both of them."

A lady said to her new maid, "Mary, we have breakfast promptly at seven every morning."

"All right, ma'am," the maid replied. "If I ain't down yet, don't wait for me."

A railroad construction foreman needed help to repair a stretch of roadbed that had been washed out by a flood. Seeing a lazy-looking fellow leaning up against a telephone post, he said, "I need some help here, Bud. Want a job?"

"How much do you pay?" the man asked.

"Oh, we usually pay a man what he's worth," the foreman replied.

"No thanks," the man retorted. "You ain't gettin' me that cheap."

Job applicant: Do you have an opening for a genius?

Interviewer: Yes, and don't slam it on the way out.

"Do you believe in life after death?" a supervisor asked his clerk.

"Yes I do, sir," she replied.

"That's good," the employer said, "because yesterday after you left early to attend your grandfather's funeral, he stopped by to see you."

"Miss Jones," said the baffled office manager, "how do you do it? You've only been here two weeks and already you're one month behind."

A customer had been trying on shoes for more than an hour and still couldn't decide which pair to buy. The shoe salesman had gone back and forth to the stockroom at least 30 times in search of something that would please her. Finally, he sat in the chair next to her and said, "Excuse me, but do you mind if I rest for a few minutes? Your feet are killing me."

Farmer: If you really want to work…I could use a right-hand man.

Vagrant: Just my luck. I'm left-handed.

The suitor drew his girlfriend's brother aside. "How would you like to earn some money?"

"Love to," the brother said. "What do you want me to do?"

"Well," said the lover, lowering his voice. "Here's a dollar. Can you get me a lock of your sister's hair."

"For $5," the brother replied, "I'll get you the whole wig."

Writers

The cub reporter was told to keep his copy short and stick to the bare facts. Sent on his first accident story, he turned in this copy: "S. White looked up the elevator shaft to see if the car was on its way down. It was. Age 45."

The newspaper editor had just been informed that a power line had fallen across Main Street in a storm. He assigned two reporters to the story. "We don't know whether the wire is live or not," he said, "so I want one of you to touch it and the other to write the story."

A minister sold a book manuscript and was dying to tell someone about it, but no one would ask. He attended a minister's convention, but still there was no chance to share his news. Finally, he was asked to lead in a closing prayer, and with his mind full of his recent accomplishment, he prayed, "O God, who also has written a Book..."

Writer: Did you know I've taken up writing as a career?

Friend: No. Have you sold anything yet?

Writer: Yes—my watch, my saxophone, and my overcoat.

Friend to writer: Don't you find writing a thankless job?

Writer: On the contrary. Everything I write is returned to me with thanks.

Bill: They tell me your son in college is quite an author. Does he write for money?

Bob: Yes, in every letter.

Author: I desire no remuneration for this poem. I merely submit it as a compliment.

Publisher: Then allow me to return the compliment.

To learn more about Harvest House books and
to read sample chapters, visit our website:

www.harvesthousepublishers.com

HARVEST HOUSE PUBLISHERS
EUGENE, OREGON